The Red Shoes
and other poems from the edge

by Deborah J. Hunter

Copyright © 2018 Deborah Hunter.
All rights reserved. No part of this publication may be reproduced, stored in a retrieval system, or transmitted, in any form or by any means, electronic, mechanical, photocopying, recording, or otherwise, except as permitted under Section 107 or 108 of the United States Copyright Act, without the written permission of the author.

ISBN 978-0-9896845-7-6

Poems included in this volume have been published in the following literary journals:
"Doomed to Repeat" — *This Land Press – 2014*
"Jazz On A Diamond Needle Hi-Fi" — *This Land Press – 2011*
"On the Occasional Beating" — *Aroostook Review – 2006*
"My Poems Are Too Loud"— *The Pedestal - 2005*
"Mama's Ferns" — *Curbside Review – 2002*
"Wild Horses" — *Another Sun (U.K) - 2001*

Performance of "Jazz On A Diamond Needle HiFi" can be seen here:
https://www.youtube.com/watch?v=_omBHktDHiI

All poems in this collection have been performed or read at festivals, slams and/or on film or stage by the poet.

Painting on the cover by Francine Campbell aka Faida
Cover & book design by Carlos Moreno

*To my daughters, Erica, Kristen and Cara.
I love you more than I can ever express.*

Contents

The Red Shoes	9
My Poems Are Too Loud	13
Imagine	15
Homage	17
March 19, 2003	19
Doomed To Repeat	20
Woman of Color	22
On Aging	24
I Don't Know Why I'm Telling You This	25
Pushin'	26
Jazz On A Diamond Needle Hi-Fi	27
Jazz Duet In Brubeck Tempo	28
Magenta	29
I Don't Write Love Poems	30
The Morning After	31
Ring of Fire	32
Teeth	33
Where Does The Blues Come From?	34
Post Trauma: After the Rape	35
Legends	36
Dream As Metaphor As Dream…	38
Mama's Ferns	40
Bruises	41
On The Occasional Beating	42
Crow's Wing	43
Wild Dog; Bluebird	44
The Last Warm Night of Autumn	45
Wolves	46
de ja vous	47
Nerve Endings Have Memories	48
Wild Horses	49
Recovery	50

THE RED SHOES
[inspired by the Hans Christian Andersen fable]

I.
She hides
red pumps
in her closet, wrapped in tissue paper,
nestled in a plain cardboard shoe box,
with her wishes and dreams,
only taking them out when she is starving,
to slide them slowly, deliciously onto her feet,
running her hands up her calves, thighs, hips,
already swaying to music in her head,
music that fills her nightmares, and
the red pumps
carry her out onto the streets,
into the neighborhoods,
where she will not be recognized,
where she finds beautiful young men
who do not know or care to know
who she is; hard, muscled bodies
who love her woman's curves.
She finds them in blues bars,
dance clubs, college taverns;
young men who are flattered
that she lets them take the lead,
lets them bury their noses
in her bosom, between her thighs;
young men with the intoxicating scent
of what could have been -
should have been - her life,
giving her a high no drug
could ever promise
as they dance - the chosen one
above her, beneath her, between
the red pumps,
challenging childhood memories,

veiling recurring visions
of what was and is and will be
that hover in the air.
She satisfies the tug
of unidentified desire,
borne out of an
undiscovered dark place,
for soul-stirring, fiery flame,
for slow-burning embers,
for the spark that ignites
bright red visions,
in red shoes.

II.
He hides
red pumps
in his closet, wrapped in tissue paper,
nestled in a plain cardboard shoe box,
with his wishes and dreams,
only taking them out when he is starving,
to slide them slowly, deliciously onto his feet,
running his hands up his calves, thighs, hips,
already swaying to music in his head,
music that sometimes makes him forget
when his father walked in
catching him in a gypsy spin;
red pumps
shining in the lamplight,
hands with red-nailed fingers fanning
this moment forever frozen, mid-step,
in red pumps,
his father, eyes wide, then narrowed
in disgust, hands clenching,
moving across the beige carpet
like a locomotive bellowing,
fist catching the side of his face,
the word, "Faggot!" echoing forever,

the red pumps
snatched so violently from his feet
that crimson streaked the beige carpet,
and these days,
behind a locked door,
he satisfies the tug
of unidentified desire,
borne out of an
undiscovered dark place,
for soul-stirring, fiery flame,
for slow-burning embers,
for the spark that ignites
bright red visions,
in red shoes.

III.
She hides
red pumps
in her closet, wrapped in tissue paper,
nestled in a plain cardboard shoe box,
with her wishes and dreams,
only taking them out when she is starving,
to slide them slowly, deliciously onto her feet,
running her hands up her calves, thighs, hips,
already swaying to music in her head,
music that is never completely silent
but is the background to her husband's curses,
accompanies her baby's cries, mixes with
the static in her brain until she wears
the red pumps
to church one Sunday morning
and dances in the main aisle
between the rows of pews
while the choir sings a song that
harmonizes with the music in her head,
music he tried to knock out
with his boot but only made louder,

until now it drowns out nearly everything else.
Now she hides
the red pumps
in her head with the music,
and in a room all her own,
she satisfies the tug
of unidentified desire,
borne out of an
undiscovered dark place,
for soul-stirring, fiery flame,
for slow-burning embers,
for the spark that ignites
bright red visions,
in red shoes.

Epilogue:
They longed
for comfort, for warmth,
to fulfill their dreams,
to escape their anguish,
and got their wish
in red shoes
the color of pomegranates,
like burnished apples,
like red-washed plums,
like …
hearts.

My Poems Are TOO LOUD

I have been reading writers of prize-winning poetry,
gracious words in soothing voices by proper poets
who lull their audiences into the lush comfort of privilege
with poems about sailboats and houses by the ocean,
cabins in the mountains, villas on the outskirts of
Rome or Athens or Paris. But, my poems are not
quiet, not suitable for prizes and literary pages.
I imagine, while filing my letters of rejection,
dark suited editors covering their ears or
slumping over their desks as my words
hit them in the chest like arrows that
I draw and release one by one.
They are befuddled by the barrage
of bellowing bullets that I discharge
from the smoking barrel of my Bic.

I am a warrior
with an infinite store of words in my arsenal,
using diplomatic discourse with just enough sting to cause a brain itch,
or vocal visuals of venomous vocabulary when necessary.

I move from horse stance
to attack pose
fingers of death
grasping my quick-on-the-draw quill.

I am lethal.
I am a warrior
with a brain
and a keyboard.
I am a catalyst on a mission
and I can't accomplish what I must
with pleasant words in a gentle voice
whispering about seagulls, ocean breezes,
and cross country train rides.

There are children who are
        Smoking, toking, snorting, shooting, leaning
        Dropping, popping, bonging, huffing, blunting
Their brains into oatmeal
While the government
Of them
By them and
For them
Wages a war
Against them.

There are women who go down on their knees
In private humiliation for the price of a hamburger
That they may purchase fresh over the counter
Rather than accept the indignation
Of waiting in a public doughnut line.

Reality exists in other dimensions for
Thousands who live on sidewalks
While their brains lie to them
With disembodied tongues
In a society that turns up its nose,
Steps over them,
Walks around them
Scrapes them from the soles of its shoes
Like dog shit left unattended.

I am a political poet.
I am a word warrior.
I am T-N-T in a petite package with a short fuse.
I cannot expound of the banalities of leisure
While people are
Shut out, shut in, shut up
Jailed in, penned in, locked down
Ignored, ignobled, interned
Frustrated, debilitated, obliterated
And I am not
   going to be quiet about it.

IMAGINE
(September 11, 2001)

Hate seems like a black hole that
sucks in all that approaches it -
like the gaping maw of the
anaconda appears to its meal -
a hollow space
extending into the shadows
swallowing and swallowing . . .

Don't you wonder?
Don't you wonder sometimes?

Constant sorrow
drips from the sky, pelts Earth's skin
drapes it in gray, conceals the sun
flows pain out into the streets
roars with a thousand voices
slices through sections of sameness
rattles windows, topples towers
steals souls, bursts into liquid flame
fuses flesh to bone, burns tunnels
of darkness that
look
like
black holes.

Don't you wonder?
Don't you wonder sometimes?

But somewhere sparks pulse
with the luminosity
of candle flames dancing
on the breath of prayer.

Don't you wonder?
Don't you wonder sometimes?

It's storming outside.
John Lennon's singing "Imagine."
I've never seen so many candles.

HOMAGE - April 19, 1995
The Bombing of the Federal Building
Oklahoma City, Oklahoma

I saw a robin the day before
and taught my child to say "bird";
eyes wide with wonder, lips an "o"
wrapped around the rolling consonant.
The grass was ripening.
Leaves were newborn.
The explosion
- wild -
and bright as the robin's red breast.
Was the sun shining?
I don't recall.

We met for lunch the day before,
had pizza with all but anchovies,
hesitated over vacation plans,
whispered conspiratorial comments
about other diners.
The sky was blue,
her dress pale yellow.
I always thought I'd go first.

He called the day before.
He'd been promoted, received a raise,
was thinking about marriage.
The azaleas flashed pink skirts;
irises spread their purple cowls.
He was proud to serve, they told us,
and we grew old then.

Sorrow creeps upon us like a cobra,
striking and recoiling.
Death was here and gone, visible

only in the faces of the children
and in the eyes of those
quaking with aftershocks.
We question and theorize,
wonder and search,
while within us grows anger
like thunder clouds
rolling over the mountains,
like shadows
following the sun,
like darkness
washing away the light,
until we are able to understand that . . .

All who are and have been
bloom in the Spring flowers,
stretch, root-heavy into the earth,
reach heavenward to the stars,
sit peacefully upon our hearts.

March 19, 2003
(the bombing of Iraq)

while I was riding to San Antonio
I watched a hawk
that looked like a hieroglyph
against a fingerpainted sky

at the same time
on the other side of the world
pyrotechnic flashes
ripped a whole in the heavens

while I was riding to San Antonio
trees fanned out across fields
on the edge of the road
like embroidered bird bones

at the same time
in a place we think of as faraway
explosions rattled walls
shook the bones of children

while I was riding to San Antonio
I saw trees gathered in a huddle
their legs a corral, their leafy arms a canopy
for cattle and their young

at the same time
in a city built on sand
mothers huddled in corners
wondering
who was the real terrorist

when I sleep tonight
I will not dream of
hawks on the wing
grassy prairies and
pastoral tranquility

Doomed to Repeat

About the 1921 Tulsa, Oklahoma Race Invasion and Massacre called Riot:
It is not our failure to remember the past that dooms us to repeat it. It is our failure to believe we are capable of the same acts.

Your disbelief blooms in slow motion,
like smoke smothering the sky,
like a death wound under white linen.

This telling of history from your too-late
perspective creates a bubble in my mind
that I cannot identify until it bursts
in my mouth into incredulous laughter.
You say you are shocked by the cruelty, but
this is how it has always been for us.
Your Tulsa is not my Tulsa.

Do you think we have always walked with
downcast eyes, heads drooping on our shoulders
and rounded back bones like wilted tulips,
speaking in hushed, inoffensive tones
so as not to be judged ripe for the noose?
This was the lesson our grandmothers taught us,
the lesson they learned from you grandfathers.

So, now, when you have accepted the Truth
of the massacre called riot, you wonder
why I am unimpressed by your outrage
at men who were the children of Indian murderers
and slave rapists, born in a country that debates
the worth of a black skin against the worth
of a brown skin against the worth
of a red skin against the worth
of a yellow skin while the scales are
weighted in favor of the white skin,

and how you cannot believe your own grandfather

committed this "small act" of terrorism when
it was his great-grandfather who auctioned black flesh,
his grandfather who engineered the Trail of Tears,
his father who rushed to claim stolen promised land.

It was your grandfather standing in the back
of a pickup truck, holding a molotov cocktail.
It was my grandmother hiding in her own house who,
a millisecond before she fled the flames of Greenwood,
saw the gleeful malice dancing in his eyes as the match flared.

Woman of Color

You imagine that I am flippant about being black
that it's something I ignore
or pretend is of no consequence.

You imagine that because I refuse to be a victim
and because I pound the heads of my brothers and sisters
with fists of furious admonition
screaming at them to
cease the blaming
stop pointing the finger
terminate the hate
and because I am able to
love a white man
befriend a white woman
cuddle a white child
that I am leaving behind
my heritage
my identity
my ancestry
that I am denying
my color
my family
my race.

The reality of who I am escapes you:
I am a woman of color.

I
talk thunder

laugh lightning
walk like a gazelle
dance like a tornado
I
make love like
a hurricane
a jungle monsoon
a tempest in a lava light
and not like
a prairie rain
Southern drizzle
Paris spring or
an English fog.

I don't dip my finger in the bowl of today to decide if I want to partake
I dive in
head first
full bodied
full out
full of expectation
I don't make mistakes
I make changes
I don't draw my hand out of the fire
until I feel the pain.
I don't back down
or look away
I will cross the line
each
time
you
draw it.

Why would I wish to trade my birthright
for a paler shade of life?

I am a colorful woman.

On Aging

My summer was fire and furious winds that
frizzed my opponents' brows, shriveled the vanity
of any oncomer who fancied himself Icarus,
new and improved.

My days of pepper passion may be passing away
into cool mornings and sunny afternoons, but
I caution those who wait for me to waste away.
They wait in vain.

The red beast called "sunset,"
haloed with the gaunt gold of acorn elders
that drape the hillside, lives at the dawn of death
and I yearn, watching it sway in dusk's cradle,
to be utterly wild.

Volcanic bubbles will push to the surface
and burp through the mud of conformity
with acrid fumes more potent than blood and furious flies.
I am not leafless yet and even winter has its bite and blow.

I Don't Know Why I'm Telling You This

I don't drink beer anymore.

I never really liked beer, but
on those happy hour evenings
when the boss was buying,
I admit I indulged;
it was free.

A time or two I had too many,
swapped boasts with the guys.
and bellied up to the pool table.
I don't even know how to rack 'em up,
but under the influence, I believed
I was a geometric genius who
could, from strategically
odd angles and curves,
sink cue balls into pockets
with professional ease.
I wanted to sing loud and
tell dirty jokes.
I wanted to kick ass and
get a cute hunk of a guy
without too much brains
and get a piece.

My brother says
I have too much testosterone.

I don't drink beer anymore.

Pushin'

I'm pushin' 50, crowdin' 49.
I'm liftin' my spirits,
raisin' my expectations.
I'm not lookin' for Mr. Right;
I'm lookin' for Mr. Hot.
I'm not settlin' for Mr. Right Now;
I deserve Mr. Everything I Want.

And I want him
in the glad season of life with zest, zip and vigor,
sometimes wind-whipped and feral,
sometimes a soothing zephyr;
and I want him
with ample lips and visionary eyes;
he can be coffee, nutmeg, cream or vanilla
as long as he's yummy, scrumptious, ambrosial;
and I want him
libidinous, my own personal satyr, "emotion in motion"
and I want him
serendipitous and zealously Zen;
and I want him
manly, majestic, powerful and proud;
and I want him
to see me as the resolution to his quest.

But most of all, I want him now.

Jazz On A Diamond Needle Hi-Fi

Mama dropped the needle and my heart jumped.
It was fascinating, titillating,
be-boppin', foot stompin', biscuit soppin',
donut dippin', daytrippin', corn sippin',
make me wanna shout, cuss somebody out;
It was without a doubt,
the most sinfully rappin', toe-tappin', thigh slappin', happenin'
     event.

It was the sun risin', moon smilin',
mamas cryin', souls dyin',
life goin' on
goin' on
goin' on.

It was
Coltrane shatterin' shackles.
Bird makin' the night air moan.
Dizzy gettin' busy with the brass.
Brubeck redefining time.
Miles moving mountains meter by meter.
Ella bouncing lightning bolts off the sky.

    {Ella Fitzgerald scat}

It was jazz.
ooh, jazz.
yeah, jazz.
It was tss-tss-tss-tss

Jazz.

Jazz Duet In Brubeck Tempo

Keyboard warriors
Square off with
Ebony rapiers and
Ivory scimitars
Parry, feint, thrust
Hide-and-seek melodies
Invent spontaneous
        Syncopations
        Variations
        Renunciations
        Reconciliations
Insinuate rapture
Hint at blue rondos
Stir a cauldron's brew
Of African dreams
Under a Turkish sun.

Magenta

Clematis lipstick
watermelon kiss after dancing
mango blush upon brown cheeks
hot, cool jazz at sunset
my name in his mouth at sunrise

I Don't Write Love Poems

I want to write a love poem about

how I know he's in the room
before I see or hear him
because the invisible thread between us
tugs at my center;

how I lift my eyes to his
and everything else falls away into mist
and we are the only two solid things
in the world;

how my skin feels an almost alarming
electrical shock
when he touches me;

how when he leans forward
I can't breathe as if my body
is preparing to die from the ecstasy
of his kiss.

I want to write a poem about Love
        but ...

The Morning After

You have just left me
smiled the smile
that I imagine
mirrors my own
only
with eyes wearier than mine.

Desires deeper than the ones we sated last night
flow restlessly beneath your still exterior
play, rewind, and play, through sleepless nights
and you wonder if you've done the right thing
if you ever have.

Ring of Fire

I know obsession,
the vise that clamps
with needful teeth of fear.

I know passion,
the self-indulgent self
that crackles just under my skin.

I don't know love.
Love flits on the edge of my vision
whispers in someone else's ears.

Teeth
(inspired by a Native American legend)

He does not know she has teeth
in her vagina
teeth
hidden deep down
waiting
silent

One night, years ago, while we slept,
his hand found its way across the vastness
of mutual self-protection.
His fingers wrapped themselves gently around mine.
I felt the teeth unclench, turn to flowing milk.

As years passed, he covered me with his shadow,
forceped what should have eased into being,
flaunted what he would not release to me.

My submission did not fill his need,
did not appease the silent commands
that must be obeyed, manifesting themselves
in threatening salutes of erect maleness
that pound against my closed teeth
breaking them, shattering resistance.

The teeth are not predatory;
but forced extraction fuels
homicidal tendencies.

The teeth slowly grow again
hidden
silent
waiting ...

Where Does The Blues Come From?

from the long, low, anguished blue note a rending soul wails
in dark so dark that a no-moon-midnight brings welcome light

blue-black tones

like wings
like flight
like night
held close then released
half notes floating
swooping, gliding
beating out a rhythm
strange to the wind
new to the ocean
old as the silence of loss

Post-Trauma: After the Rape

I am amazed at this tick-tocking
of daily life that plods on with
the meandering sameness that
resolves nothing, reveals even less.

I am amazed that I lift up and
put down one foot after the other
on cold hard cement,
even when I am indoors.

I am amazed that when I look
down at the ground
I do not see myself lying there,
a freeze-dried relic of who I thought I was
and not enough tears to restore me.

Legends

Movies I saw, TV I watched, books I read,
taught me that a prince with
your good looks and bulging bank account
would save me,
put me in a big house and a big car,
hold me in powerful, gentle arms,
drive out memories of other arms,
arms that pinned me down,
wrenched me open,
imprisoned my soul in its dark night.
       There are dragons here.

Movies I saw, TV I watched, books I read,
taught me that it was my destiny
to save a woman with your beauty and raw pain.
You were my princess in distress.
I wanted to put you in a big house and a big car,
hold you in my powerful, gentle arms,
drive away the dragons that you pretended weren't there.
       I thought I could buy you safety.
       I thought I could love you free.

I am lost in this house,
my sanctuary, my fortress,
but, it is my prison, my dungeon
of nightmares: strange faces,
insistent hands clamp to my knees,
dilate and scrape me out.
Dragons
breathe fire, tear my skin,
push between my thighs,
inside me, rip out

the life I was supposed to have,
the me I was supposed to be
is running down my legs,
puddling at my feet ...
It's just dragons in my dreams
and dragons aren't real.
They're an illusion.
Are you an illusion, too?

It's one o'clock in the morning.
I'm sitting on the edge of our bed
waiting for you to come home
because I failed you.
> I was too selfish, not selfish enough;
> expected too much, didn't expect enough;
> talked too much, didn't talk enough;
> couldn't be what you needed.

I am reminded of the stone giant who,
after all that he loved was ripped from his hands,
sat alone, desolate, in utter anguish and said,
"They look like good, strong hands, don't they?"
I'm looking down at my hands now,
hands that could not hold onto you,
feeling his despair,
feeling my human-ness
because
I cannot light
the growing darkness in your soul.
I cannot slay
the dragons in your dreams.

Dream as Metaphor as Dream …

She was born in water
With the knowledge that fire swallowed dreams
And expelled them as soot and ash.

When the playground children shouted,
"Y tu mama tambien,"
The words rattled and rankled.
Fire had come when her mother was a girl.
It had come to her grandmother.
It would come to her.

Fire stalked the women in her family,
Its long red-orange tentacles
Lapped at generation after generation
Who were taught their deliverance
Lay in keeping the flames
Banked down to smoldering embers.

Unguarded, the coals flashed
Out of their confinement
In an uncontrolled blaze,
So no one in her house had dreams
Only night terrors that lingered on
In the bold, bright face of day.

In her musings, she placed her feet
firmly on the earth
breathed with the wind
closed her eyes
felt her feet grow roots that

pushed into the dirt
stretching long and thin
seeking the cool wet giver of life.

While she stood
planted
a bird perched in her nest of hair
sang to her,
"Fi-re, fi-re, fi-re.
Wa-ter, wa-ter, wa-ter."
Her roots drank their fill,
the bird flew away,
she opened her eyes.

She was born in water
and believed
it would be her salvation.

Mama's Ferns

Mama's ferns in the corner of the livingroom
slowly close when she and her husband come home.
Their leaves fold into tiny praying hands.

No doors slam tonight.
No voices swell into hoarse shouts,
slurred expletives, red and purple flashes.
Not tonight.

But I lie awake and listen anyway,
vigilant until I hear mild, obliging murmurs
and the sighs of a mattress glad to be of service.

Bruises

she can't see rainbows
only
collapsed splotches of color
unfolding themselves
backwards

On the Occasional Beating

She never hit me where it showed
except by accident.
      "I-will-kill-you!"

One time the belt buckle snapped free
lunged forward
like a cobra uncoiled, hit me
across the nose.
      "I-will-kill-you!"

Blood dripped
roused a forgotten nightmare
of a pillow pressed down
pressed down
flailing arms and legs.
      "I-will-kill-you!"

It was as effective
as a strait jacket
I lived inside
the lines
she drew for me
heel to toe
slack face
bland eyes
arms to my side.

      "I-will-kill-you!"

was all it took
most of the time.

Crow's Wing
(for Velma)

I find a crow's wing in a field.
Fanned open it is iridescent in sunlight;
awesome under the glow of the moon.

My friend who was full of fear
has been haunted by blue black crows
who speak to her in dreams and
dance across her unmowed lawn.

Lately, though,
she has tried to listen to the crows
in her dreams and in her yard, especially
since one came to her on her patio and
looked her straight in the eye.

His gaze was wise as he chastised her.
"We crows," it said, in no uncertain terms,
"do not shrink back from the unpleasant."
"We crows," it said, "take life as it comes."

"We crows are the great carrion feeders
who clean up what others leave; clear away
odoriferous decay that smothers light
and keeps life from growing where it should."

And she finally understands because this
is what she has done all her life.
"We crows are the blue black curiosities
of this world, my friend." And for the first time,
in a long time, she knows who she is.

Wild Dog, Bluebird
(A Richard Bay painting)

Wild Dog dances with Death
under cloudy skies,
demented, in pain,
his dog life confirmed.
And the bluebird turns its back.

Wild Dog licks his wounds,
ceases his mad dance,
learns that touch can heal
more than caresses,
stares Death in the eye,
hunkers down, whispers,
"I'm ready for you."

Death's power is lost.
Wild dog paws the earth,
Bluebird rides on his
shoulder, scowls at death.

The Last Warm Night of Autumn

Our meeting;
dew of spring and warmth
that blazed
into summer passion
and settled
into autumn's turning.

But

When the cold came,
the bitter winter of
loneliness,
I knew
I had already seen
the last warm night of autumn.

Wolves

You claim to be a lone wolf
loping in solitude,
daring fear, cheating death,
howling in the mist.
But I know the truth.

Your soul cowers in the shadows
hunkering down in the bitterness
of icy memories.
You appear feral,
but are tame at heart,
craving acceptance,
a wild thing
needing love.

And I …
I claim to be a child of the sun
leader of the pack,
calling to the wind,
fiercely self-sufficient.
But you know the truth.

My soul shrinks from the crowds
seeking the shade of obscurity,
the quiet of solitude.
I appear feral
but am tame at heart,
craving acceptance,
a wild thing
needing love.

I keep your secret, as you keep mine.

Wolves mate for life
and
the lone wolf is a legend.

de ja vous

i
swirled into a whirlpool
struggled in the undertow
gasped for air

i thought i saw you twice yesterday

Nerve endings have memories

I know this because mine remember him.
My whole body remembers him.
I have had others and

my lips register a vague reminiscence
when I am near the one whose kiss
melted my resolve into spring puddles.

My torso tugs a little toward the one who
wrapped me in chiseled arms, pulled me
against his great, beveled chest, granted me
temporary sanctuary.

Then there's the one who makes the parting,
where my thighs don't quite touch, sweat
with the heat of wanting what he so generously gave.

The one who makes my whole body remember
sneaks into my dreams,
creeps around the edges of my thoughts.
For him, the little nerve endings dance and squeal in delight,
bouncing against one another in a frenzied mosh pit of expectancy.

But the last time we made love felt like the last time.
Our lips went cold when the kisses ended.
There was no ecstasy in the release.
The heat between us dissipated like steam on the rise.

The little nerve endings are forgetting.
I am the one keeping the memories alive.
Not much longer, though, I know, so
I await the numb dullness of amnesia and
the absence of full-body effervescence.

Wild Horses

I know nothing about wild horses only
that their ferocity and beauty thrive
in the impetuous autonomy of non-restraint.
The stallion rears up, snorts, dances on two legs.
Basic blind instinct moves mares into his harem.

I loved a man once who summoned women with
a sideward glance, a crooked smile, chomped
at the bit of belonging, crowded phone numbers
and names into the corral of short-term memory.

I know nothing about wild horses
only that they thrive
in the impetuous autonomy of non-restraint.

Recovery
(for the loved ones I've lost in death)

I move through the hazy days
Wanting only those clear nights
Those nights you come to me in dreams
Put your hand to my cheek,
lean your head on mine

You're never far from me, it's said
And sometimes I truly believe it
When I feel you standing just behind me
And I turn to tell you something

Sometimes, anger and sorrow
Fill me up, overflow into words
That I don't want to take back
And enough tears to salt the roads of winter.

I am missing you more than
Anyone can understand, but
Sometimes, the curtain lifts.

Hope is an open door and
I know the choice is mine.

Acknowledgements

Thank you to: my writers' groups for their feedback and for being my constant, faithful, cheering sections; Francine Ringold, former editor of *Nimrod Literary Journal*, who was the first editor of note to publish my work and became my dear friend; the late Raymond and Nancy Feldman, for their encouragement and all others who ever gave me my first chance to be a published poet, performer, actor, playwright, director, workshop facilitator and whatever else I can think of to try next.

Deborah J. Hunter, poet, performance artist and actor, has facilitated poetry workshops and worked as a poet-in-residence in schools and community programs since 1997. She was a 2013 Oklahoma Poet Laureate nominee. *Urban Tulsa Weekly* listed her as one of its "Hot 100 Picks" for 2007, naming her "Poet Extraordinaire". She has served on the Advisory Board of the Oklahoma Center for Poets and Writers and, more recently, on the selection committee for the Oklahoma Poet Laureate.

Deborah's poetry has appeared in numerous literary journals and anthologies, including *Nimrod International Journal, Another Sun* (U.K.), *Aroostook Review, Art Focus Oklahoma*, and *A Voice Was Sounding*. She was presented with the $5000 Jingle Feldman Artist Award in 2000.

Hunter is also a community activist who advocates for the homeless and those with mental illnesses by serving on several boards toward that cause and participating in trainings on mental health issues. She was a contributing author to the 2013 academic text, *Violence and Abuse in Society: Understanding a Global Crisis*.

Deborah has been acting in local stage productions since 2000, had a small role in an independent film and performs her one-woman spoken word performance piece, *Amazons, Gypsies and Wandering Minstrels*, which gives voice to women who are marginalized because of mental illness, substance use, abuse and homelessness.

The Red Shoes
and other poems from the edge

by **Deborah J. Hunter**

www.ingramcontent.com/pod-product-compliance
Lightning Source LLC
Chambersburg PA
CBHW050448010526
44118CB00013B/1731